1 Introduction

In late-2008, short-term nominal interest rates in the U.S. fell to their effective "zero lower bound" (see Bernanke *et al.*, 2004). Since standard Gaussian term structure models do not rule out the possibility of negative model-implied yields, they provide a poor approximation to the behavior of nominal yields when the lower bound is binding (Kim and Singleton, 2012; Christensen and Rudebusch, 2013; Bauer and Rudebusch, 2013). Kim and Singleton (2012) find that shadow-rate models in the spirit of Black (1995) successfully capture yield-curve properties observed near the zero lower bound. However, arbitrage-free multi-factor versions of these models tend to be computationally intractable (Christensen and Rudebusch, 2013). Gorovoi and Linetsky (2004) show that bond prices in a one-factor shadow-rate model can be computed analytically by an eigenfunction expansion, but their approach does not generalize to multiple dimensions. Kim and Singleton (2012) and Ichiue and Ueno (2007) successfully estimate shadow-rate models with up to two factors, but they compute bond prices using discretization schemes that are subject to the curse of dimensionality. Christensen and Rudebusch (2013) use a yield formula proposed by Krippner (2012) to estimate shadow-rate Nelson-Siegel models with up to three factors, but Krippner's derivation deviates from the usual no-arbitrage approach. Bauer and Rudebusch (2013) evaluate bond prices by Monte Carlo simulation for given model parameters from an unconstrained Gaussian term structure model, but they do not estimate a shadow-rate version of the model due to the computational burden.

This paper develops and applies a new technique for fast and accurate approximation of arbitrage-free zero-coupon bond yields in multi-factor Gaussian shadow-rate models of the term structure of interest rates. The computational complexity of the method does not increase with the number of yield curve factors, and, empirically, it produces yields that are accurate to within about half a basis point. The method is sufficiently fast to estimate a flexible, arbitrage-free, three-factor term structure model in which the shadow rate follows a Gaussian process. For illustration purposes, I estimate such a model by quasi-maximum likelihood on a sample of U.S. Treasury yields, using the unscented Kalman filter to account for the non-linear mapping between factors and yields.

2 Model

Consider first the standard, continuous-time N-factor Gaussian term structure model. In particular, let $W_t^{\mathbb{P}}$ be N-dimensional standard Brownian motion on a complete probability space $(\Omega, \mathcal{F}, \mathbb{P})$ with canonical filtration $\{\mathcal{F}_t\}_{t \geq 0}$. Assume there is a pricing measure $\mathbb{Q}$ on $(\Omega, \mathcal{F})$ that is equivalent to $\mathbb{P}$, and denote by $W_t^{\mathbb{Q}}$ Brownian motion under $\mathbb{Q}$ as derived from Girsanov's Theorem (Karatzas and Shreve, 1991). Suppose N latent factors (or states) representing uncertainty underlying term-structure securities follow the multivariate Ornstein-Uhlenbeck process

$$dX_t = (K_0^\mu + K_1^\mu X_t)dt + \Sigma dW_t^\mu \tag{1}$$

were $\mu \in \{\mathbb{P}, \mathbb{Q}\}$. Let the short rate be

$$r_t = \rho_0 + \rho_1 \cdot X_t. \tag{2}$$

Then by definition, the arbitrage-free time t price of a zero-coupon bond maturing at time T is given by

$$P_t^T = \mathbf{E}_t^{\mathbb{Q}} \left[\exp\left(-\int_t^T r_s \, ds\right) \right] \tag{3}$$

with associated zero-coupon bond yield

$$y_t^T = -\frac{\log P_t^T}{T-t}. \qquad (4)$$

Bond prices (and hence yields) can equivalently be defined in terms of forward rates:

$$P_t^T = \exp\left(-\int_t^T f_t^s \, ds\right) \quad \Leftrightarrow \quad f_t^T = -\frac{d}{dT}\log P_t^T \qquad (5)$$

where f_t^T denotes the instantaneous time T forward rate effective at time t.

Since X_t is a Gaussian process (Karatzas and Shreve, 1991), it follows from (2) that the short rate r_t takes on strictly negative values with strictly positive probability. To modify the model in a way that accounts for the zero lower bound on nominal yields, Black (1995) proposes to think of r_t as a *shadow* short rate (and, analogously, of P_t^T, y_t^T, and f_t^T as shadow bond price, shadow yield, and shadow instantaneous forward rate, respectively) and define the *observed* short rate as the shadow rate censored at zero:

$$\underline{r}_t = \max\{r_t, 0\}. \qquad (6)$$

With the observed short rate $\underline{r}_t$ in place of the shadow rate r_t, the observed bond price $\underline{P}_t^T$, yield $\underline{y}_t^T$, and instantaneous forward rate $\underline{f}_t^T$ are then defined as in (3)–(5).

3 Parameterizing the Lower Bound

The theoretical argument for a lower bound *at zero* on the nominal short rate (and hence on nominal yields) is based on arbitrage between bonds and currency (Black, 1995). In practice, the two assets may not be perfect substitutes for reasons such as convenience, default risk, or legal requirements. This may push the empirical lower bound into slightly negative or slightly positive territory. The derivations in Section 2 are easily modified to accommodate a lower bound at $r_{\min} \neq 0$. In particular, suppose

$$\underline{r}_t = \max\{r_t, r_{\min}\} = r_{\min} + \max\{r_t - r_{\min}, 0\}.$$

Then,

$$\begin{aligned}
\underline{y}_t^T &= -\frac{1}{T-t}\mathbf{E}_t^{\mathbb{Q}}\left[\exp\left(-\int_t^T \underline{r}_s\, ds\right)\right] \\
&= r_{\min} - \frac{1}{T-t}\mathbf{E}_t^{\mathbb{Q}}\left[\exp\left(-\int_t^T \max\{r_s - r_{\min}, 0\}\, ds\right)\right].
\end{aligned}$$

The last term is equal to the expression for the yield when the lower bound is zero, except that $r_{\min}$ is subtracted from the shadow rate. Therefore, since $r_s = \rho_0 + \rho_1 \cdot X_s$, when the lower bound is nonzero we can compute zero-coupon yields as if the bound were zero, with $\rho_0 - r_{\min}$ in place of ρ_0, and then add $r_{\min}$ to the final result. The lower bound $r_{\min}$ can be set to a specific value based on a priori reasoning, or treated as a free parameter in estimation.

4 Bond Price Computation

A central task in term-structure modeling is the (analytical and/or numerical) computation of arbitrage-free bond prices (and hence yields) based on equation (3). Section 4.1 reviews the standard approach using differential equations formalized by Duffie and Kan (1996), best suited to affine models. While it can be adapted to the shadow-rate framework, it loses much of its analytical tractability, and becomes computationally infeasible as the number of factors increases. Section 4.2 discusses an alternative method proposed by Krippner (2012). It defines a pseudo–forward rate that satisfies the lower bound (though differs from the arbitrage-free forward rate), and uses relationship (5) to approximate bond prices. Finally, Section 4.3 proposes a new approximation technique for yields in the shadow-rate model based on the expansion of a cumulant-generating function.

4.1 Partial Differential Equation

Like any conditional expectation of an $\mathcal{F}_T$-measurable random variable, $e^{-\int_0^t r_s \, ds} P_t^T$ (the time t price of a zero-coupon bond maturing at time T in the unconstrained Gaussian model, discounted to time 0) follows a martingale under $\mathbb{Q}$. This is an immediate consequence of the definition of a martingale, after an application of the Law of Iterated Expectations. Using Itō's Lemma and the Martingale Representation Theorem, we can therefore represent P_t^T by the function $D(X_t, T-t)$, where D solves the partial differential equation (PDE)

$$D_\tau(x,\tau) = D_x^\top(x,\tau)(K_0^{\mathbb{Q}} + K_1^{\mathbb{Q}} x) + \frac{1}{2}\text{tr}\big(\Sigma^\top D_{xx}(x,\tau)\Sigma\big) - (\rho_0 + \rho_1 \cdot x)D(x,\tau) \quad (7)$$

with boundary condition $D(x,0) = 1$. Using a separation-of-variables argument, it can be verified that

$$D(x,\tau) = e^{A(\tau) + B(\tau) \cdot x} \quad (8)$$

solves (7), where A and B in turn solve ordinary differential equations (ODEs) in terms of the model parameters,

$$A'(\tau) = K_0^{\mathbb{Q}} \cdot B(\tau) + \frac{1}{2} B(\tau)^\top \Sigma \Sigma^\top B(\tau) - \rho_0 \quad (9)$$

$$B'(\tau) = (K_1^{\mathbb{Q}})^\top B(\tau) - \rho_1 \quad (10)$$

with $A(0) = 0$, $B(0) = 0$. Reducing problem (7) to the system of ODEs (9)–(10) simplifies the numerical computation of bond prices substantially as it reduces the dimensionality of the problem from $N + 1$ to 1 (the time dimension). Direct computation reveals that

$$B(\tau) = ((K_1^{\mathbb{Q}})^{-1})^{\top}(I_N - e^{(K_1^{\mathbb{Q}})^{\top}\tau})\rho_1, \qquad (11)$$

assuming $K_1^{\mathbb{Q}}$ is invertible.

A PDE analogous to (7) can be set up for the observed bond price in the shadow-rate model, $\underline{P}_t^T$. The only required modification is to replace the expression for the shadow short rate, $r = \rho_0 + \rho_1 \cdot x$, by that for the observed short rate, $\underline{r} = \max\{\rho_0 + \rho_1 \cdot x, 0\}$. Unfortunately, when this non-linearity is introduced, the separation-of-variables procedure no longer applies, and no solution as straightforward as (8) is available. It is possible to solve the modified version of (7) directly by numerical methods. This is the approach taken by Kim and Singleton (2012). It requires discretizing τ and x on a multidimensional grid, which is computationally intensive and subject to the curse of dimensionality. Kim and Singleton (2012) therefore do not estimate models with more than two factors.

4.2 Forward Rate Approximation

Krippner (2012) proposes an alternative approach to computing yields in shadow-rate models, which is implemented empirically by Christensen and Rudebusch (2013). It is based on an approximation to the forward rate $\underline{f}_t^T$. Substituting for $\underline{P}_t^T$ from the shadow-rate version of (3), and differentiating, we obtain

$$\underline{f}_t^T = \mathbf{E}_t^{\mathbb{Q}}\left[\frac{e^{-\int_t^T \underline{r}_s\, ds}}{\underline{P}_t^T}\underline{r}_T\right] = \mathbf{E}_t^{\mathbb{Q}_T}[\underline{r}_T] = \mathbf{E}_t^{\mathbb{Q}_T}[\max\{r_T, 0\}] \qquad (12)$$

where $\underline{\mathbb{Q}}_T$, defined by the Radon-Nikodym derivative

$$\frac{d\underline{\mathbb{Q}}_T}{d\mathbb{Q}} = \frac{e^{-\int_0^T \underline{r}_s\, ds}}{\mathbf{E}^{\mathbb{Q}}\left[e^{-\int_0^T \underline{r}_s\, ds}\right]},$$

is referred to as the "T-forward measure." Equation (12) says that today's time T forward rate is equal to today's expectation under the T-forward measure of the time T short rate. It can be verified directly from (12) and the Law of Iterated Expectations that $\underline{f}_t^T$ is a martingale under $\underline{\mathbb{Q}}_T$ (note that $\underline{r}_T \equiv \underline{f}_T^T$ by definition). Note also that (12) implies that the forward rate is subject to the same lower bound (6) as the short rate, by monotonicity of the mathematical expectation.

Analogously,

$$f_t^T = \mathbf{E}_t^{\mathbb{Q}}\left[\frac{e^{-\int_t^T r_s\, ds}}{P_t^T} r_T\right] = \mathbf{E}_t^{\mathbb{Q}_T}[r_T] \tag{13}$$

expresses the *shadow* forward rate as the expectation under the *shadow T-forward measure* of the future *shadow* short rate. Again, f_t^T is a martingale under $\mathbb{Q}_T$. Unlike the observed forward rate, it is not, however, constrained to be non-negative.

The distribution of the shadow forward rate f_t^T under $\mathbb{Q}_T$ can be derived more explicitly. First, from (5) and (8),

$$f_t^T = -A'(T-t) - B'(T-t) \cdot X_t.$$

Therefore, by Itō's Lemma and the Martingale Representation Theorem,

$$f_T^T = f_t^T - \int_t^T B'(T-s)^\top \Sigma\, dW_s^{\mathbb{Q}_T}. \tag{14}$$

Thus, f_T^T is Gaussian under $\mathbb{Q}_T$ conditional on $\mathcal{F}_t$, with

$$\mathbf{E}_t^{\mathbb{Q}_T}[f_T^T] = f_t^T$$
$$\operatorname{Var}_t^{\mathbb{Q}_T}[f_T^T] = \mathbf{E}_t^{\mathbb{Q}_T}\left[\left(\int_t^T B'(T-s)^\top \Sigma \, dW_s^{\mathbb{Q}_T}\right)^2\right]$$
$$= \underbrace{\rho_1^\top \left(\int_t^T e^{(K_1^\mathbb{Q})^\top (T-s)} \Sigma \Sigma^\top e^{K_1^\mathbb{Q}(T-s)} \, ds\right) \rho_1}_{\omega(T-t)}. \tag{15}$$

The final equality uses the Itō Isommetry and (11).[1]

Krippner (2012) takes advantage of this distributional property of $f_T^T \equiv r_T$. He defines a pseudo–forward rate as a hybrid between observed forward rate (12) and shadow forward rate (13):

$$\underline{f}_t^T = \mathbf{E}_t^{\mathbb{Q}}\left[\frac{e^{-\int_t^T r_s \, ds}}{P_t^T} \underline{r}_T\right] = \mathbf{E}_t^{\mathbb{Q}_T}[\underline{r}_T] = \mathbf{E}_t^{\mathbb{Q}_T}[\max\{r_T, 0\}]. \tag{16}$$

This is the expectation under the *shadow* T-forward measure of the *observed* time T short rate (while the shadow-model-implied forward rate consistent with the absence of arbitrage is given by (12) as the expectation under the *observed* T-forward measure of the *observed* time T short rate).[2] This rate is, by monotonicity, subject to lower bound (6). It is, moreover, relatively straightforward to compute: Lemma A.1 in

---

[1] The integral in (15) has the same form as (A.2) in Appendix A and therefore can be computed analytically as in (A.3).

[2] Krippner (2012) motivates his derivation in terms of options on shadow bonds. To derive (16) from his equations (12) and (13), replace the call option price by

$$\mathbf{E}_t^{\mathbb{Q}}\left[e^{-\int_t^T r_s \, ds} \max\left\{\mathbf{E}_T^{\mathbb{Q}}\left[e^{-\int_T^{T+\delta} r_s \, ds}\right] - 1, 0\right\}\right].$$

Then interchange the limit operations and expectation, and evaluate.

Appendix A implies that

$$\underline{f}_t^T = \mathbf{E}_t^{\mathbb{Q}^T}\left[\max\{f_T^T, 0\}\right] = f_t^T \Phi\left(\frac{f_t^T}{\omega(T-t)}\right) + \omega(T-t)\phi\left(\frac{f_t^T}{\omega(T-t)}\right). \quad (17)$$

This is formula (32) in Krippner (2012).[3] Note from (17) that $\underline{f}_t^T/f_t^T \to 1$ as f_t^T increases or $\omega(T-t)$ decreases. That is, as the lower bound becomes less binding, the wedge between $\underline{f}_t^T$ and the shadow forward rate f_t^T (which is the arbitrage-free forward rate in a Gaussian model without lower bound) shrinks.

Zero-coupon bond prices $\underline{P}_t^T$ and yields $\underline{y}_t^T$ can be approximated by substituting $\underline{f}_t^T$ from (17) into (5) and (4).

4.3 Cumulants

Since the PDE approach to pricing bonds in shadow-rate models becomes computationally intractable as the number of factors increases, and the approach proposed by Krippner (2012) relies on a forward rate that is not equal to the arbitrage-free forward rate, I propose a new cumulant-based technique to approximating yields in Gaussian shadow-rate models.

The quantity $\log \underline{P}_t^T = \log \mathbf{E}_t^{\mathbb{Q}}\left[\exp\left(-\int_t^T \underline{r}_s\, ds\right)\right]$ appearing in the shadow-rate version of (4) is the conditional cumulant-generating function[4] under $\mathbb{Q}$, evaluated at

---

[3] Krippner (2012) uses the parametrization proposed by Chen (1995) and hence obtains his formula (31) for ω as a special case of (15). Similarly, the results derived by Christensen and Rudebusch (2013) are (essentially) special cases of (15) and (17) under their Nelson-Siegel parametrization (where some of the derivations must be modified appropriately to account for the fact that their matrix $K_1^{\mathbb{Q}}$ is singular). Don Kim (personal communication) independently derives the general expression for ω in (15) by generalizing Krippner's (2012) computations directly.

[4] The cumulant-generating function of a random variable X is defined as the logarithm of its moment-generating function (for example, see Severini, 2005).

-1, of the random variable $\underline{R}_t^T \equiv \int_t^T \underline{r}_s \, ds$. It has the series representation

$$\log \mathbf{E}_t^{\mathbb{Q}} \left[\exp\left(-\underline{R}_t^T\right) \right] = \sum_{j=1}^{\infty} (-1)^j \frac{\kappa_j^{\mathbb{Q}}}{j!} \tag{18}$$

where $\kappa_j^{\mathbb{Q}}$ is the jth cumulant of $\underline{R}_t^T$ under $\mathbb{Q}$. An approximation to the zero-coupon yield $\underline{y}_t^T$ can therefore be computed based on a finite number of terms in the series in (18). Below, I consider the first-order approximation

$$\underline{\tilde{y}}_t^T = \frac{1}{\tau} \kappa_1^{\mathbb{Q}} = \frac{1}{T-t} \mathbf{E}_t^{\mathbb{Q}} \left[\int_t^T \underline{r}_s \, ds \right] \tag{19}$$

and the second-order approximation

$$\underline{\tilde{\tilde{y}}}_t^T = \frac{1}{T-t} \left(\kappa_1^{\mathbb{Q}} - \frac{1}{2} \kappa_2^{\mathbb{Q}} \right) = \frac{1}{T-t} \left(\mathbf{E}_t^{\mathbb{Q}} \left[\int_t^T \underline{r}_s \, ds \right] - \frac{1}{2} \mathrm{Var}_t^{\mathbb{Q}} \left[\int_t^T \underline{r}_s \, ds \right] \right) \tag{20}$$

where I make use of the fact that the first two cumulants of any random variable coincide with its first two centered moments.[5]

The first-order approximation (19) is equivalent to the method proposed independently and contemporaneously by Ichiue and Ueno (2013). I present it here both for comparison and to assess its relative performance in Section 5 below. I will, however, mostly focus on the second-order approximation (20), which I argue is particularly promising a priori because it is exact in the Gaussian benchmark case.[6] It can therefore be expected to perform well both for short maturities (where the higher-order terms in (18) are relatively small), and for long maturities as long as $\mathbb{Q}_t[r_T < 0]$ is small for large T (in which case $\underline{r}_t = \max\{r_t, 0\}$ will behave approximately like a

---

[5]Higher-order approximations following the same general logic are possible, but they are increasingly computationally costly while generating decreasing marginal benefits in terms of precision.

[6]The third- and higher-order cumulants of a Gaussian random variable are zero, so that (20) coincides with the usual affine-Gaussian yield formula in that case.

Gaussian process over sufficiently long horizons). Indeed, empirically, the second-order approximation turns out to be highly accurate across maturities both during normal times and when rates are low (see Section 5).

4.3.1 Computation of the First Moment

Evaluating the first- and second-order approximations (19) and (20) to zero-coupon yields requires computation of the first two cumulants (equivalently, centered moments) of $\underline{R}_t^T = \int_t^T \underline{r}_s \, ds$. This subsection will be concerned with the first moment. As an initial step,

$$\mathbf{E}_t^{\mathbb{Q}} \left[\int_t^T \underline{r}_s \, ds \right] = \int_t^T \mathbf{E}_t^{\mathbb{Q}} \left[\underline{r}_s \right] ds \tag{21}$$

by an application of Fubini's Theorem. Since $\underline{r}_s = \max\{r_s, 0\}$ and $r_s \sim N(\mu_{t \to s}, \sigma_{t \to s}^2)$ with known expressions for $\mu_{t \to s}$ and $\sigma_{t \to s}^2$ in terms of the model parameters (as shown in Appendix A), it follows from Lemma A.1 in Appendix A that

$$\mathbf{E}_t^{\mathbb{Q}} \left[\int_t^T \underline{r}_s \, ds \right] = \int_t^T \left[\mu_{t \to s} \Phi \left(\frac{\mu_{t \to s}}{\sigma_{t \to s}} \right) + \sigma_{t \to s} \phi \left(\frac{\mu_{t \to s}}{\sigma_{t \to s}} \right) \right] ds \tag{22}$$

where ϕ and Φ denote the standard normal probability density function (pdf) and cumulative distribution function (cdf), respectively. That is, we can compute $\mathbf{E}_t^{\mathbb{Q}}[\underline{r}_s]$ analytically up to the standard normal cdf, which software such as Matlab is able to evaluate precisely and efficiently. The first cumulant of $\underline{R}_t^T$ can then be computed by numerical integration of $\mathbf{E}_t^{\mathbb{Q}}[\underline{r}_s]$ over the time dimension, as in (22).

4.3.2 Computation of the Second Moment

Once we know the first moment of $\underline{R}_t^T = \int_t^T \underline{r}_s \, ds$, it remains to evaluate

$$\mathbf{E}_t^{\mathbb{Q}}\left[\left(\int_t^T \underline{r}_s \, ds\right)^2\right] = 2 \int_t^T \int_t^s \mathbf{E}_t^{\mathbb{Q}}[\underline{r}_u \underline{r}_s] \, du \, ds \qquad (23)$$

where the equality uses Fubini's Theorem and symmetry of the integrand. Since $\underline{r}_u = \max\{r_u, 0\}$ and $\underline{r}_s = \max\{r_s, 0\}$, and (r_u, r_s) are jointly normally distributed with mean $(\mu_{t\to u}, \mu_{t\to s})$, variances $(\sigma_{t\to u}^2, \sigma_{t\to s}^2)$, and covariance $\sigma_{t\to u\times s}$ (see Appendix A), we obtain from Lemma A.2 in Appendix A:

$$\mathbf{E}_t^{\mathbb{Q}}\left[\left(\int_t^T \underline{r}_s \, ds\right)^2\right]$$
$$= 2 \int_t^T \int_t^s \Bigg\{ (\mu_{t\to u}\mu_{t\to s} + \sigma_{t\to u\times s})\Phi_2^d\left(-\varsigma_{t\to u}, -\varsigma_{t\to s}; \chi_{t\to u\times s}\right)$$
$$+ \sigma_{t\to s}\mu_{t\to u}\phi\left(\varsigma_{t\to s}\right)\Phi\left(\frac{\varsigma_{t\to u} - \chi_{t\to u\times s}\varsigma_{t\to s}}{\sqrt{1 - \chi_{t\to u\times s}^2}}\right)$$
$$+ \sigma_{t\to u}\mu_{t\to s}\phi\left(\varsigma_{t\to u}\right)\Phi\left(\frac{\varsigma_{t\to s} - \chi_{t\to u\times s}\varsigma_{t\to u}}{\sqrt{1 - \chi_{t\to u\times s}^2}}\right)$$
$$+ \sigma_{t\to u}\sigma_{t\to s}\sqrt{\frac{1 - \chi_{t\to u\times s}^2}{2\pi}}\phi\left(\sqrt{\frac{\varsigma_{t\to u}^2 - 2\chi_{t\to u\times s}\varsigma_{t\to u}\varsigma_{t\to s} + \varsigma_{t\to s}^2}{1 - \chi_{t\to u\times s}^2}}\right) \Bigg\} du \, ds \qquad (24)$$

where $\varsigma_{t\to j} = \frac{\mu_{t\to j}}{\sigma_{t\to j}}$, $j \in \{u, s\}$, $\chi_{t\to u\times s} = \frac{\sigma_{t\to u\times s}}{\sigma_{t\to u}\sigma_{t\to s}}$, and Φ_2^d denotes the decumulative bivariate normal cdf.

That is, we can compute $\mathbf{E}_t^{\mathbb{Q}}[\underline{r}_u \underline{r}_s]$ analytically up to the *bivariate* normal cdf, and we can then integrate this expression numerically over u and s to obtain the second cumulant of $\underline{R}_t^T$.

4.3.3 Numerical Implementation

The following steps summarize the approximation procedure for zero-coupon yields for a given set of parameters $(K_0^{\mathbb{Q}}, K_1^{\mathbb{Q}}, \rho_0, \rho_1, \Sigma)$ and state vector X_t:

1. Compute the conditional mean and covariance matrix of (r_u, r_s), for $u, s \geq t$, using (A.4) and (A.5).

2. Using the results from step 1, compute $\mathbf{E}_t^{\mathbb{Q}}[\underline{r}_s]$ and $\mathbf{E}_t^{\mathbb{Q}}[\overline{r}_u \overline{r}_s]$, for $u, s \geq t$, as described in 4.3.1 and 4.3.2.

3. Integrate $\mathbf{E}_t^{\mathbb{Q}}[\underline{r}_s]$ numerically to obtain $\mathbf{E}_t^{\mathbb{Q}}[\underline{R}_t^T]$, and integrate $\mathbf{E}_t^{\mathbb{Q}}[\overline{r}_u \overline{r}_s]$ numerically to obtain $\mathbf{E}_t^{\mathbb{Q}}[(\overline{R}_t^T)^2]$.

4. Using the moments computed in step 3, approximate $\underline{y}_t^T$ by $\tilde{y}_t^T$ or $\tilde{\tilde{y}}_t^T$ as defined in (19) and (20).

In terms of numerical implementation, step 1 is straightforward. Step 2 requires evaluation of the univariate and bivariate normal cdf's. A high-precision, efficient approximation to the univariate normal cdf is built into most computational software packages, so numerically evaluating the first integrand does not pose a challenge. For the bivariate normal cdf, I implement a vectorized version of an algorithm proposed by Genz (2004) which achieves double machine precision.[7] Step 3 is straightforward in principle, though a favorable tradeoff between precision and computational burden requires careful choice of quadrature rule and grid. I use composite Gauss-Legendre and Gauss-Lobatto rules with 2–20 points per maturity (and corresponding product rules for the double integral in (24)), selected to evaluate $\tilde{y}_t^T$ or $\tilde{\tilde{y}}_t^T$ to an approximate minimum numerical precision of $1/100^{\text{th}}$ of a basis point. With fully vectorized Matlab

---
[7] Matlab's built-in function mvncdf uses adaptive numerical integration to compute the bivariate normal cdf. This is slower by several orders of magnitude than the algorithm I use.

code,[8] I am able to evaluate a full representative sample of model-implied zero coupon yields (approximately 20 years of monthly data across eight maturities) within a fraction of a second.

Note that the complexity of the algorithm does not depend on the number of yield curve factors N, so it is not subject to the curse of dimensionality in the same way that some other methods are.[9]

For illustration purposes, in Appendix B I apply the second-order approximation method to estimate a three-factor shadow-rate model of the U.S. Treasury term structure.

5 Accuracy of Yield Approximation Methods

Section 4.3 argued intuitively that the second-order yield approximation (20) should be relatively precise. This section quantifies that claim. To get an initial sense of the relative numerical accuracy, I consider the stylized model used for illustration by Gorovoi and Linetsky (2004), and replicated for the same purpose in Krippner (2012). It is a one-factor model with $\rho_0 = 0.01$, $\rho_1 = 1$, $K_0^{\mathbb{Q}} = 0$, $K_1^{\mathbb{Q}} = -0.1$, and $\Sigma = 0.02$. Gorovoi and Linetsky (2004) derive model-implied yield curves for states $X_t \in \{-0.06, -0.02, -0.01, 0\}$ corresponding to shadow short rates $r_t = \{-0.05, -0.01, 0, 0.01\}$. The four panels of Figure 1 plot the model-implied yield curves for each initial state. Within each panel, I compare four different yield approximation schemes: Solving PDE (7) numerically (which, in a one-factor setting,

---

[8]That is, without for-loops that grow with the number of quadrature points, states, dates, or maturities in the sample.

[9]The general approximation methodology I propose has its own curse of dimensionality in that the second-order approximation is substantially more computationally involved than the first-order approximation (and any higher-order approximation will be substantially more involved than the second-order approximation). In practice, the second-order approximation appears to strike an acceptable balance between precision and computational complexity for many cases of interest, see Section 5 below.

is computationally feasible and can be considered the "exact" solution for comparison purposes), Krippner's (2012) approach described in Section 4.2, and the first- and second-order approximations proposed in Section 4.3. As the figure shows, the second-order approximation matches the exact PDE solution most closely, and consistently across states. The yield approximation error is uniformly less than one basis point. The first-order approximation generally overstates yields (an implication of the alternating nature of series expansion (18)), with approximation errors increasing both in yield maturity and the level of the shadow short rate (in both cases, the first-order approximation is off by an increasingly large convexity adjustment arising from Jensen's inequality). Krippner's (2012) method generally undershoots yields, and is relatively more accurate when the shadow short rate is higher. Why this is the case can be seen intuitively by comparing the $\mathbb{Q}$-measure expressions for the arbitrage-free forward rate (12) and Krippner's (2012) approximate forward rate (16): While both use the same time T short rate $\underline{r}_T$, Krippner's (2012) formula discounts by the *shadow* rate rather than the observed short rate. This means the discount factor tends to be larger than it should be when $\underline{r}_T$ is low, reducing the covariance between discount factor and $\underline{r}_T$, and thus lowering the expectation of their product, f_t^T.

To compare the relative performance of the different yield approximations in a more realistic empirical setting, I use the estimated model parameters and smoothed states from Appendix B.3 to compute model-implied yield curves for all dates in the sample.[10] Since this is a three-factor model, solving PDE (7) numerically is no longer practicable. I therefore replace this benchmark by a simulated yield $\hat{\underline{y}}_t^T$ that consistently estimates the true yield $\underline{y}_t^T$ based on $n = 1{,}000{,}000$ randomly drawn

---

[10]The sample consists of end-of-month observations from January 1990 through December 2012.

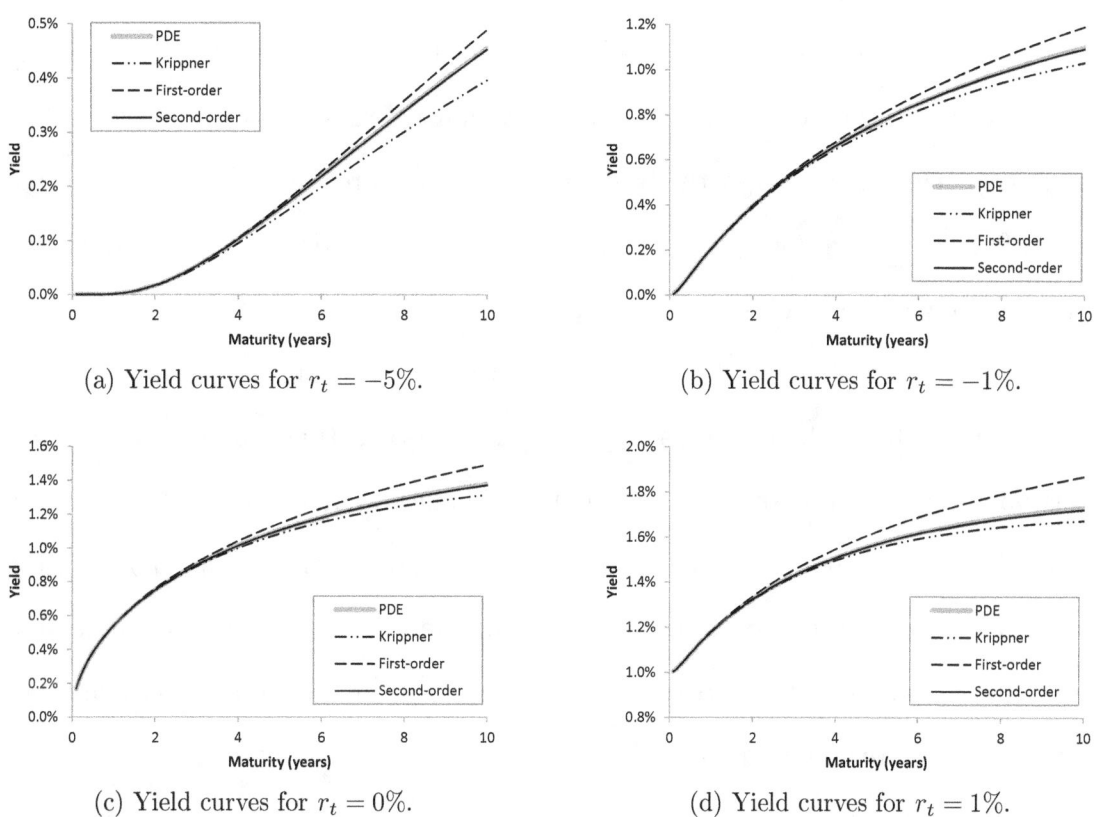

(a) Yield curves for $r_t = -5\%$.

(b) Yield curves for $r_t = -1\%$.

(c) Yield curves for $r_t = 0\%$.

(d) Yield curves for $r_t = 1\%$.

Figure 1: Yield curves (zero-coupon yield against maturity in years) implied by a one-factor shadow-rate model with $\rho_0 = 0.01$, $\rho_1 = 1$, $K_0^{\mathbb{Q}} = 0$, $K_1^{\mathbb{Q}} = -0.1$, and $\Sigma = 0.02$. The different panels correspond to different initial shadow short rates. Within each panel, the yield curve is computed using four methods: Numerical solution of PDE (7), Krippner's (2012) approach described in Section 4.2, and the first- and second-order approximations proposed in Section 4.3.

short-rate paths per sample date.[11,12] Table 1 shows the mean simulation error of $\hat{\underline{y}}_t^T$, and the root-mean-square errors (RMSE) against $\hat{\underline{y}}_t^T$ of the yield $\underline{y}_t^T$ computed by Krippner's (2012) method, the first-order approximation $\tilde{\underline{y}}_t^T$ defined in (19), and the second-order approximation $\tilde{\tilde{\underline{y}}}_t^T$ defined in (20). The table is divided into two panels. The top panel shows errors for the sub-sample Jan 1990–Nov 2008 (when interest rates were at normal levels), and the bottom panel shows errors for the sub-sample Dec 2008–Dec 2012 (when the lower bound on nominal yields was binding at the short end of the yield curve). All methods are generally more precise at shorter maturities. As the first column in both panels shows, the simulated yields are accurate to within approximately one fifth of a basis point at the ten-year maturity point. As shown in the second column of the tables, Krippner's (2012) method produces ten-year yields that are accurate to about one basis point during normal times, and to within four basis points when the lower bound is binding. While the first-order method is more accurate when rates are low (the bottom panel), its errors remain substantial at the long end. The second-order method, the final column in the tables, produces ten-year yields that are accurate to approximately half a basis point, both during normal times and when the lower bound is binding.

To further illustrate the time-varying relative performance of the three approximation schemes, Figure 2 plots the difference over time between the simulated ten-year yield and the three approximated yields. Krippner's (2012) method and the second-order approximation appear to be equally precise in the first few years of the sample,

---

[11]I simulate (1) under $\mathbb{Q}$ based on moments (A.1)–(A.2) on a uniformly-spaced grid with $\Delta t = 1/360$. For each simulated path i, I compute $\underline{R}_t^T(i) = \int_t^T \underline{r}_s(i)\, ds$ by the trapezoidal method. I then define $\hat{\underline{P}}_t^T = \frac{1}{n}\sum_{i=1}^n \exp(-\underline{R}_t^T(i))$ and $\hat{\underline{y}}_t^T = -\frac{1}{T-t}\log \hat{\underline{P}}_t^T$. The simulation error for $\hat{\underline{P}}_t^T$ is computed as $n^{-1/2}$ times the sample standard deviation, and the simulation error for $\hat{\underline{y}}_t^T$ is derived from the simulation error for $\hat{\underline{P}}_t^T$ by the delta method.

[12]The simulation takes several hours to complete for the given parameter estimates and smoothed states. This approach would not, therefore, be feasible as part of an estimation strategy.

Maturity	se($\hat{\underline{y}}_t^T$)	RMSE($\underline{y}_t^T$)	RMSE($\tilde{\underline{y}}_t^T$)	RMSE($\tilde{\tilde{\underline{y}}}_t^T$)
6m	0.04	0.04	0.05	0.04
1y	0.06	0.06	0.18	0.06
2y	0.09	0.10	0.88	0.10
3y	0.12	0.14	2.26	0.13
4y	0.14	0.18	4.22	0.15
5y	0.16	0.27	6.60	0.17
7y	0.19	0.47	12.22	0.21
10y	0.21	0.93	21.81	0.35

(a) Sub-sample Jan 1990–Nov 2008

Maturity	se($\hat{\underline{y}}_t^T$)	RMSE($\underline{y}_t^T$)	RMSE($\tilde{\underline{y}}_t^T$)	RMSE($\tilde{\tilde{\underline{y}}}_t^T$)
6m	0.01	0.01	0.01	0.01
1y	0.02	0.04	0.04	0.02
2y	0.05	0.19	0.33	0.05
3y	0.07	0.51	1.07	0.07
4y	0.10	0.94	2.31	0.09
5y	0.12	1.42	3.99	0.12
7y	0.15	2.43	8.38	0.23
10y	0.17	3.87	16.63	0.52

(b) Sub-sample Dec 2008–Dec 2012

Table 1: The mean standard error of simulated yields $\hat{\underline{y}}_t^T$ ($n = 1{,}000{,}000$ draws per sample date) for the model estimated in Appendix B, and the root-mean-square errors (RMSE) against the simulated yields of Krippner's (2012) yield approximation $\underline{y}_t^T$, the first-order yield approximation $\tilde{\underline{y}}_t^T$, and the second-order yield approximation $\tilde{\tilde{\underline{y}}}_t^T$. All errors are in basis points.

with fluctuations presumably largely due to simulation error.[13] The discrepancy between simulated yield and Krippner's (2012) method increases over time as the level of yields declines, and exceeds five basis points by December 2012. The discrepancy between simulated yield and second-order approximation remains small and appears to show little systematic variation over time, perhaps trending up modestly towards the end of the sample. The first-order approximation has a large negative discrepancy initially, which shrinks over time but remains at a high absolute level even at the end of the sample.

Figure 2 also confirms that, just like in the simple one-factor model in Figure 1, the approximation errors under Krippner's (2012) method and the first-order scheme are largely systematic (rather than mere noise), in that the first-order approximation overstates arbitrage-free yields while Krippner's (2012) method tends to understate them.

In sum, the analysis above suggests that, empirically, the second-order yield approximation $\tilde{\underline{y}}_t^T$ is accurate to within about one half of a basis point at maturities up to ten years, both during normal times and when the lower bound is binding. The approximation error is one order of magnitude smaller than both the model-implied observation error in yields (see Table 3) and the next best approximation method proposed by Krippner (2012). In contrast, the first-order approximation is acceptable at most at the very short end of the yield curve.

To add perspective, the approximation error in $\tilde{\underline{y}}_t^T$ is no greater than commonly accepted fitting error in the derivation of constant-maturity zero-coupon bond yields from observed coupon-bearing Treasuries (e.g., Gürkaynak et al., 2006). This puts the second-order approximation roughly on par with the numerical accuracy achieved

---

[13] Recall that when there is no lower bound, both methods produce yields equal to the exact arbitrage-free yield. In the early 1990s, the overall level of yields was sufficiently high for the effect of the lower bound to be negligible.

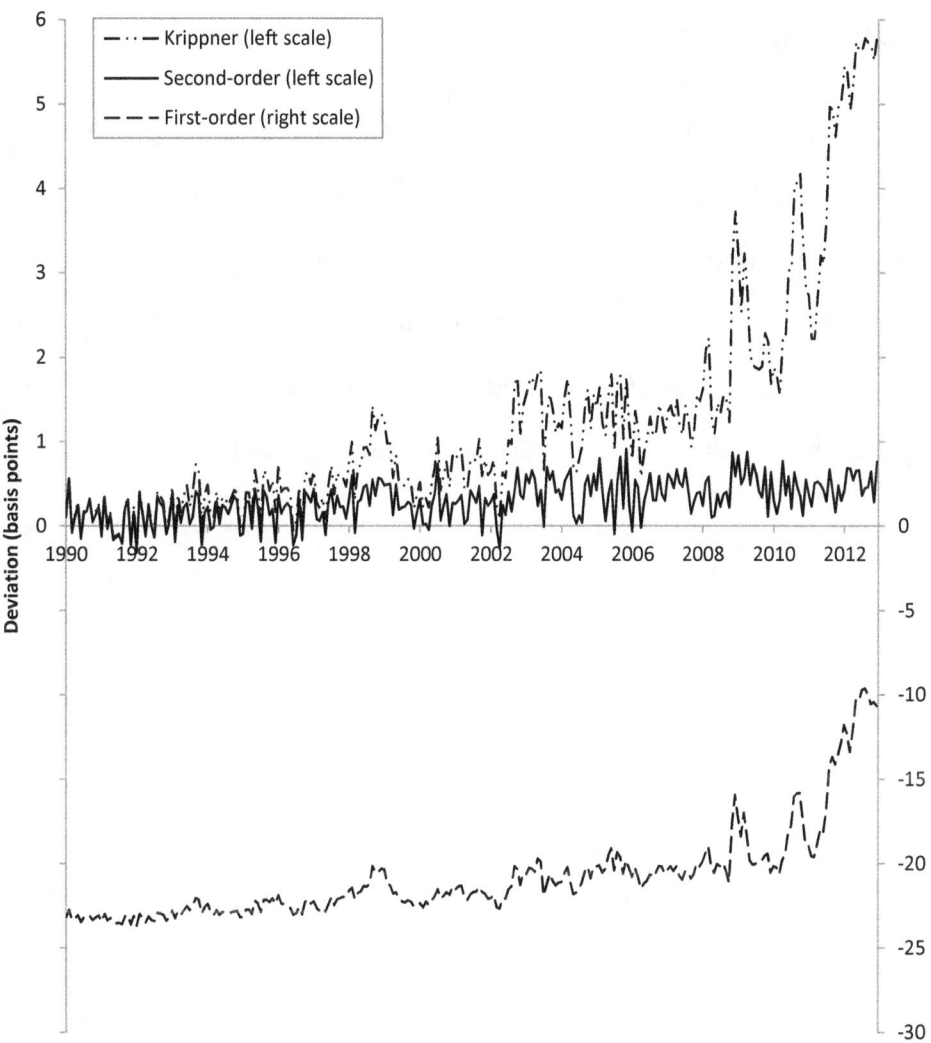

Figure 2: Deviation from simulated ten-year yield $\hat{\underline{y}}_t^{t+10}$ of Krippner's (2012) yield approximation $\underline{y}_t^{t+10}$, the first-order yield approximation $\tilde{\underline{y}}_t^{t+10}$, and the second-order yield approximation $\tilde{\tilde{\underline{y}}}_t^{t+10}$. Model parameters and filtered states are taken from Appendix B.

by "exact" bond pricing methods in standard affine models, to the extent that they rely on numerical methods (say, to solve the system of ODEs (9)–(10)).[14]

6 Conclusion

This paper develops an approximation to arbitrage-free zero coupon bond yields in Gaussian shadow-rate term structure models. The complexity of the scheme does not depend on the number of factors. Further, I demonstrate that the method is computationally feasible by estimating a three-factor shadow-rate model of the U.S. Treasury yield curve. Based on Monte Carlo simulation, I also show that the yield approximation is approximately as precise as conventional approaches that are considered to be "exact."

---

[14]Empirically, the second-order approximation $\tilde{\underline{y}}_t^T$ is exact to an absolute tolerance of approximately 5×10^{-5} (see Table 1). The default tolerance for numerical methods in Matlab is typically between 10^{-4} and 10^{-6}, depending on the complexity of the method.

A Useful Mathematical Results

A.1 Moments of X_t

Consider the continuous time stochastic process X_t defined in (1). The following derivations hold under both the $\mathbb{P}$-measure and the $\mathbb{Q}$-measure, hence for notational simplicity I will suppress dependence of moments and parameters on the measure. Since X_t is a Gaussian process, all its finite-dimensional distributions are Gaussian (Karatzas and Shreve, 1991). In particular, for $u, s \geq t$, the vectors (X_u, X_s) are jointly conditionally Gaussian, with

$$\mathbf{E}_t[X_u] = e^{K_1(u-t)} X_t + (I_N - e^{K_1(u-t)}) K_1^{-1} K_0 \tag{A.1}$$

$$\mathrm{Cov}_t[X_u, X_s] = \int_t^{u \wedge s} e^{K_1(u-v)} \Sigma \Sigma^\top e^{K_1^\top(s-v)}\, dv. \tag{A.2}$$

If K_1 is invertible, the integral on the right-hand side of (A.2) can be evaluated analytically using integration by parts and formula (10.2.15) in Hamilton (1994),

$$\mathrm{vec}(\mathrm{Cov}_t[X_u, X_s]) \tag{A.3}$$
$$= (K_1 \oplus K_1)^{-1} \mathrm{vec}(e^{K_1(u-t)} \Sigma \Sigma^\top e^{K_1^\top(s-t)} - e^{K_1(u-u\wedge s)} \Sigma \Sigma^\top e^{K_1^\top(s-u\wedge s)}),$$

where "$\oplus$" denotes the Kronecker sum. Since r_t as defined in (2) is a linear function of the Gaussian random vector X_t, it is itself Gaussian, with

$$\mu_{t \to u} = \mathbf{E}_t[r_u] = \rho_0 + \rho_1 \cdot \mathbf{E}_t[X_u] \tag{A.4}$$

and

$$\sigma_{t \to u \times s} = \mathrm{Cov}_t[r_u, r_s] = \rho_1^\top \mathrm{Cov}_t[X_u, X_s] \rho_1. \tag{A.5}$$

A.2 Moments of Censored Gaussian Random Variables

This section derives two useful mathematical results involving the moments of censored Gaussian random variables.

Lemma A.1. *If $X \sim N(\mu, \sigma^2)$, then*

$$\mathbf{E}[\max\{X, 0\}] = \mu \Phi\left(\frac{\mu}{\sigma}\right) + \sigma \phi\left(\frac{\mu}{\sigma}\right)$$

where Φ denotes the standard normal cdf, and ϕ denotes the standard normal pdf.

Proof. First, note that

$$\mathbf{E}[\max\{X, 0\}] = \mu + \sigma \mathbf{E}\left[\max\left\{\frac{X - \mu}{\sigma}, -\frac{\mu}{\sigma}\right\}\right]. \tag{A.6}$$

Thus, it only remains to compute $\mathbf{E}[\max\{Z, a\}]$ where Z is a standard normal random variable, for arbitrary $a \in \mathbb{R}$. By direct computation of the integral defining the expectation,

$$\mathbf{E}[\max\{Z, a\}] = a\Phi(a) + \frac{1}{\sqrt{2\pi}} \int_a^\infty z \exp\left(-\frac{1}{2}z^2\right) dz, \tag{A.7}$$

where Φ is the standard normal cdf. Further,

$$\int_a^\infty z \exp\left(-\frac{1}{2}z^2\right) dz = \left[-\exp\left(-\frac{1}{2}z^2\right)\right]_a^\infty = \exp\left(-\frac{1}{2}a^2\right) = \sqrt{2\pi}\phi(a). \tag{A.8}$$

Recursively substituting from (A.8) into (A.7), and finally into (A.6), establishes the result. □

Lemma A.2. *If*

$$\begin{pmatrix} X_1 \\ X_2 \end{pmatrix} \sim N\left[\begin{pmatrix} \mu_1 \\ \mu_2 \end{pmatrix}, \begin{pmatrix} \sigma_1^2 & \sigma_{12} \\ \sigma_{12} & \sigma_2^2 \end{pmatrix}\right]$$

then

$$\mathbf{E}[\max\{X_1,0\}\max\{X_2,0\}] = (\mu_1\mu_2 + \sigma_{12})\Phi_2^d(-\varsigma_1,-\varsigma_2;\chi)$$

$$+ \sigma_2\mu_1\phi(\varsigma_2)\Phi\left(\frac{\varsigma_1 - \chi\varsigma_2}{\sqrt{1-\chi^2}}\right) + \sigma_1\mu_2\phi(\varsigma_1)\Phi\left(\frac{\varsigma_2 - \chi\varsigma_1}{\sqrt{1-\chi^2}}\right)$$

$$+ \sigma_1\sigma_2\sqrt{\frac{1-\chi^2}{2\pi}}\phi\left(\sqrt{\frac{\varsigma_1^2 - 2\chi\varsigma_1\varsigma_2 + \varsigma_2^2}{1-\chi^2}}\right) \qquad (A.9)$$

where $\varsigma_j = \frac{\mu_j}{\sigma_j}$, $j \in \{1,2\}$, $\chi = \frac{\sigma_{12}}{\sigma_1\sigma_2}$, ϕ *denotes the univariate standard normal pdf,* Φ *denotes the univariate standard normal cdf,* $\phi_2(z_1,z_2;\chi)$ *denotes the bivariate normal pdf when both variables have zero means, unit variances, and correlation* χ, *and* Φ_2 *and* Φ_2^d *denote the corresponding cumulative and decumulative bivariate Gaussian distribution functions, where in particular* $\Phi_2^d(z_1,z_2;\chi) = 1 - \Phi(z_1) - \Phi(z_2) + \Phi_2(z_1,z_2;\chi)$.

Proof. Write

$$\mathbf{E}\left[\max\{X_1,0\}\max\{X_2,0\}\right]$$
$$= \sigma_1\sigma_2\mathbf{E}\left[\max\left\{\frac{X_1-\mu_1}{\sigma_1},-\frac{\mu_1}{\sigma_1}\right\}\max\left\{\frac{X_2-\mu_2}{\sigma_2},-\frac{\mu_2}{\sigma_2}\right\}\right]$$
$$+ \mu_2\mathbf{E}\left[\max\{X_1,0\}\right] + \mu_1\mathbf{E}\left[\max\{X_2,0\}\right] - \mu_1\mu_2. \qquad (A.10)$$

The second and third terms can be evaluated using Lemma A.1. For the first term, it suffices to be able to compute $\mathbf{E}\left[\max\{Z_1,a\}\max\{Z_2,b\}\right]$ for random variables Z_1 and Z_2 that are bivariate normal with zero means, unit variances, and correlation χ, and for arbitrary $a,b \in \mathbb{R}$. Using the properties of ϕ_2, this expectation can be expanded as follows:

$$
\begin{aligned}
&\mathbf{E}\left[\max\{Z_1,a\}\max\{Z_2,b\}\right] \\
&= \int_{-\infty}^{\infty}\int_{-\infty}^{\infty} \max\{z_1,a\}\max\{z_2,b\}\,\phi_2(z_1,z_2;\chi)\,dz_1\,dz_2 \\
&= ab\int_{-\infty}^{b}\int_{-\infty}^{a} \phi_2(z_1,z_2;\chi)\,dz_1\,dz_2 + a\int_{b}^{\infty}\int_{-a}^{\infty} z_2\phi_2(z_1,z_2;-\chi)\,dz_1\,dz_2 \\
&\quad + b\int_{-b}^{\infty}\int_{a}^{\infty} z_1\phi_2(z_1,z_2;-\chi)\,dz_1\,dz_2 + \int_{b}^{\infty}\int_{a}^{\infty} z_1z_2\phi_2(z_1,z_2;\chi)\,dz_1\,dz_2. \quad (A.11)
\end{aligned}
$$

The first double integral is simply $\Phi_2(a,b;\chi)$, the bivariate normal cdf. The second and third double integrals correspond to expected values of truncated bivariate normal random variables, and the last integral is the expected cross product of a truncated bivariate normal random vector. These expected values are known up to the univariate standard normal cdf and the bivariate normal cdf, respectively (see Rosenbaum, 1961). Using the formulas in Rosenbaum (1961) to evaluate the integrals in (A.11), and substituting into (A.10), we obtain (A.9) after simplification. □

B Empirical Implementation

This appendix empirically estimates a three-factor Gaussian shadow-rate term structure model using the yield approximation methodology proposed in Section 4.3. The main purpose is to demonstrate the computational tractability of the method in the context of a realistic application. For more in-depth discussion and empirical analysis, see Kim and Priebsch (2013).

B.1 Data

I use end-of-month zero-coupon U.S. Treasury yields from January 1990 through December 2012, for maturities of 6 months, 1–5, 7, and 10 years. I derive the 6-month yield from the corresponding T-bill quote, while longer-maturity zero yields are extracted from the CRSP U.S. Treasury Database using the unsmoothed Fama and Bliss (1987) methodology.[15]

I augment the yield data with survey forecasts from Blue Chip, interpolated to constant horizons of 1–4 quarters (available monthly), as well as annually out to 5 years and for 5-to-10 years (available every six months).[16] Model-implied survey forecasts are subject to the same lower-bound constraint as yields,[17] but their computation is substantially simpler: Forecasters report their expectation of the *arithmetic mean* of future observed short rates, $\mathbf{E}_t^{\mathbb{P}} \left[\frac{1}{\tau} \int_t^{t+\tau} \max\{r_s, 0\} \, ds \right]$. This is exactly (19) with the data-generating measure $\mathbb{P}$ in place of pricing measure $\mathbb{Q}$. Therefore, the first-order method described in Section 4.3 produces *exact* model-implied survey forecasts. Intuitively, unlike yields, survey forecasts are not subject to compounding, so

---

[15]I am grateful to Anh Le for providing the code for this procedure.

[16]As discussed by Kim and Orphanides (2005), this potentially leads to more precise estimates of the parameters governing the data-generating distribution $\mathbb{P}$.

[17]This follows from equivalence of the measures $\mathbb{P}$ and $\mathbb{Q}$, and more fundamentally from the absence of arbitrage.

there are no higher-order Jensen's inequality terms to consider.

B.2 Filtering and Estimation

Since the statistical properties of the term structure model laid out in Section 2 are formulated in terms of the latent state vector X_t, but the data actually observed by the econometrician consist of yields, y_t, and survey expectations, z_t (see Appendix B.1), I set up a joint estimation and filtering problem to obtain estimates of the model's parameters $\theta = (K_0^{\mathbb{P}}, K_1^{\mathbb{P}}, K_0^{\mathbb{Q}}, K_1^{\mathbb{Q}}, \rho_0, \rho_1, \Sigma)$.[18] When discretely sampled at intervals $\Delta t > 0$, the state vector X follows a first-order Gaussian vector autoregression,

$$X_{t+\Delta t} = m_{0,\Delta t} + m_{1,\Delta t} X_t + \varepsilon_t \tag{B.1}$$

where $\varepsilon_t \sim N(0, \Omega_{\Delta t})$, and $m_{0,\Delta t}$, $m_{1,\Delta t}$, and $\Omega_{\Delta t}$ can be computed from (A.1) and (A.2). Equation (B.1) represents the *transition equation* of the filtering problem.

Next, denote by $H_y : \mathbb{R}^N \times \Theta \mapsto \mathbb{R}_+^{M_Y}$ the (non-linear) mapping from states X and parameters θ to model-implied yields y, and by $H_z : \mathbb{R}^N \times \Theta \mapsto \mathbb{R}_+^{M_z}$ the analogous mapping from states and parameters to model-implied survey forecasts z. For estimation purposes, I compute H_y through the second-order approximation (20), and H_z through the exact first-order method discussed in Appendix B.1. To simplify notation, denote the stacked mapping $(H_y^\top, H_z^\top)^\top$ by H. If we assume that all yields and survey expectations are observed with iid additive Gaussian errors, we obtain the *observation equation*

$$\begin{pmatrix} y_t \\ z_t \end{pmatrix} = H(X_t) + e_t. \tag{B.2}$$

---

[18] See Duan and Simonato (1999) for an early reference discussing this approach towards term structure model estimation.

Together, equations (B.1) and (B.2) form a non-linear filtering problem.

The simple (linear) Kalman filter—optimal when measurement and observation equation are linear and all shocks are Gaussian—has been modified in a number of ways to accommodate nonlinearity as in (B.2). The *unscented Kalman filter*, proposed by Julier *et al.* (1995), aims to deliver improved accuracy and numerical stability relative to the more traditional *extended Kalman filter*, without substantially increasing the computational burden.[19,20] The algorithm is described in detail in Wan and van der Merwe (2001). As a by-product of the filtering procedure, it conveniently produces estimates of the mean and covariance matrix of (y_t, z_t) conditional on the econometrician's information set as of time $t-1$. I use these to set up a quasi–maximum likelihood function based on (B.2),[21] which I maximize numerically to obtain estimates of the parameters θ as well as their asymptotic standard errors (following Bollerslev and Wooldridge, 1992).

B.3 Estimation Results

To achieve econometric identification of the parameters θ in light of invariant transformations resulting in observationally equivalent models with different parameters (see Dai and Singleton, 2000), I follow Joslin *et al.* (2011) and impose the normalizations $\rho_1 = (1, \ldots, 1)^\top$, $K_0^{\mathbb{Q}} = 0$, $K_1^{\mathbb{Q}}$ is diagonal and therefore completely determined by its ordered eigenvalues $\lambda^{\mathbb{Q}}$, and Σ is lower triangular.

I estimate the model on the data set described in Appendix B.1, using the quasi–maximum likelihood (QML) procedure discussed in Appendix B.2. Table 2 displays the estimated model parameters $\hat{\theta}$, as well as their asymptotic standard errors.

Table 3 shows the QML-estimated standard deviations of the measurement errors

---

[19] A detailed treatment of the unscented Kalman filter, and a comparison to the extended Kalman filter, can be found in Wan and van der Merwe (2001).

[20] Christoffersen *et al.* (2012) and Wu (2010) confirm that the unscented Kalman filter performs

ρ_0	0.0738	$r_{\min}$	0.0010		
	(0.0043)		(0.0001)		
$\lambda^{\mathbb{Q}}$	−0.1038	Σ	0.0268		
	(0.0226)		(0.0084)		
	−0.3566		−0.0324	0.0416	
	(0.1177)		(0.0110)	(0.0295)	
	−0.8574		0.0068	−0.0397	0.0090
	(0.2876)		(0.0100)	(0.0302)	(0.0007)
$K_0^{\mathbb{P}}$	−0.0193	$K_1^{\mathbb{P}}$	−0.4679	−0.3415	0.3785
	(0.0052)		(0.1574)	(0.1490)	(0.6798)
	−0.0099		−0.5752	−1.1881	−1.1875
	(0.0224)		(0.6303)	(1.1335)	(0.5740)
	0.0278		0.8908	1.3060	0.3990
	(0.0233)		(0.6982)	(1.0641)	(1.3561)

Table 2: Quasi–maximum likelihood parameter estimates (asymptotic standard errors) for the three-factor shadow-rate model.

in yields and survey variables (e_t in equation (B.2)). The average yield error is 8 basis points, and the average error in surveys is 21 basis points. For both yields and surveys, errors follow a U-shaped pattern, being largest at the short and long ends.

Figure 3 plots the model-implied shadow short rate r_t over the sample period, based on the states implied by the Kalman smoother (that is, incorporating all information up to December 2012, the end of the sample). The shadow rate turned negative in December 2008, after the FOMC established a target federal funds rate range of 0 to 0.25 percent and the effective lower bound became binding, and has stayed negative through the end of the sample.

---

better than the extended Kalman filter in the specific setting of term structure model estimation.

[21] This estimation approach is described and analyzed in Lund (1997).

Maturity	σ_Y	Maturity	σ_Z
6m	0.0017	1q	0.0014
1y	0.0014	2q	0.0002
2y	0.0006	3q	0.0009
3y	0.0003	4q	0.0014
4y	0.0004	2y	0.0028
5y	0.0003	3y	0.0026
7y	0.0006	4y	0.0027
10y	0.0015	5y	0.0031
Average	0.0008	5y–10y	0.0034
		Average	0.0021

Table 3: Estimated standard deviations of observation errors in yields, σ_Y, and survey forecasts, σ_Z.

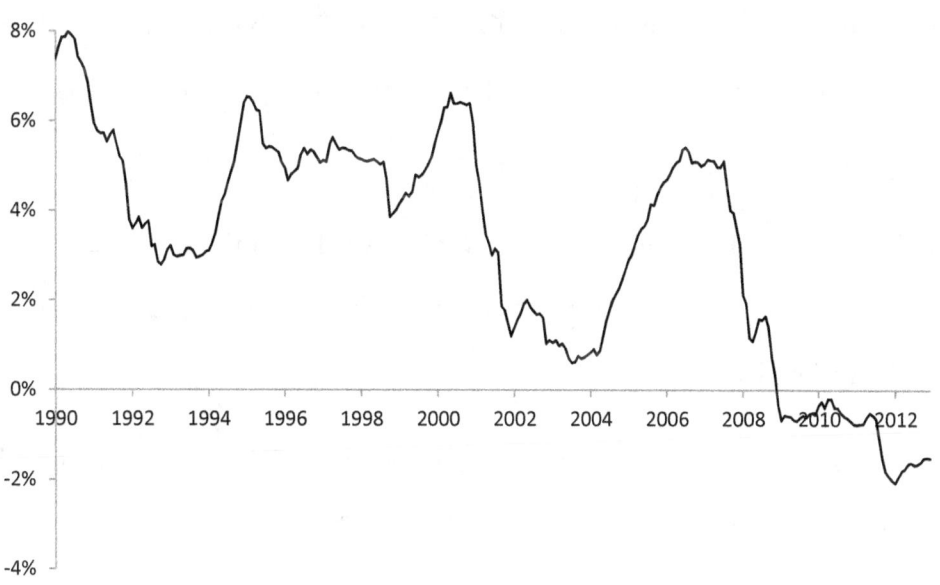

Figure 3: Model-implied shadow short rate r_t based on smoothed states $X_{t|T}$.

References

Bauer, M., and Rudebusch, G. (2013), "Monetary Policy Expectations at the Zero Lower Bound," Working Paper, Federal Reserve Bank of San Francisco

Bernanke, B., Reinhart, V., and Sack, B. (2004), "Monetary Policy Alternatives at the Zero Bound: An Empirical Assessment," *Brookings Papers on Economic Activity*, 2:1–100

Black, F. (1995), "Interest Rates as Options," *Journal of Finance*, 50(5):1371–1376

Bollerslev, T., and Wooldridge, J. (1992), "Quasi–Maximum Likelihood Estimation and Inference in Dynamic Models with Time-Varying Covariances," *Econometric Reviews*, 11(2):143–172

Chen, R. (1995), "A Two-Factor, Preference-Free Model for Interest Rate Sensivite Claims," *Journal of Futures Markets*, 15(3):345–372

Christensen, J., and Rudebusch, G. (2013), "Estimating Shadow-Rate Term Structure Models with Near-Zero Yields," Working Paper, Federal Reserve Bank of San Francisco

Christoffersen, P., Dorion, C., Jacobs, K., and Karoui, L. (2012), "Nonlinear Kalman Filtering in Affine Term Structure Models," CREATES Research Paper 2012-49, Aarhus University

Dai, Q., and Singleton, K. (2000), "Specification Analysis of Affine Term Structure Models," *Journal of Finance*, 60(5):1943–1978

Duan, J.-C., and Simonato, J.-G. (1999), "Estimating and Testing Exponential-

Affine Term Structure Models by Kalman Filter," *Review of Quantitative Finance and Accounting*, 13:111–135

Duffie, D., and Kan, R. (1996), "A Yield-Factor Model of Interest Rates," *Mathematical Finance*, 6:369–406

Fama, E., and Bliss, R. (1987), "The Information in Long-Maturity Forward Rates," *American Economic Review*, 77(4):680–692

Genz, A. (2004), "Numerical Computation of Rectangular Bivariate and Trivariate Normal and t Probabilities," *Statistics and Computing*, 14:251–260

Gorovoi, V., and Linetsky, V. (2004), "Black's Model of Interest Rates as Options, Eigenfunction Expansions and Japanese Interest Rates," *Mathematical Finance*, 14(1):49–78

Hamilton, J. (1994), *The Time Series Analysis*, Princeton University Press

Ichiue, H., and Ueno, Y. (2007), "Equilibrium Interest Rate and the Yield Curve in a Low Interest Environment," Bank of Japan Working Paper

——— **(2013)**, "Estimating Term Premia at the Zero Bound: An Analysis of Japanese, U.S., and U.K. Yields," Bank of Japan Working Paper No. 13-E-8

Joslin, S., Singleton, K., and Zhu, H. (2011), "A New Perspective on Gaussian Dynamic Term Structure Models," *Review of Financial Studies*, 24(3):926–970

Julier, S., Uhlmann, J., and Durrant-Whyte, H. (1995), "A New Approach for Filtering Nonlinear Systems," in *Proceedings of the American Control Conference*, pp. 1628–1632

Karatzas, I., and Shreve, S. (1991), *Brownian Motion and Stochastic Calculus*, Graduate Texts in Mathematics Series, Springer, London

Kim, D., and Orphanides, A. (2005), "Term Structure Estimation with Survey Data on Interest Rate Forecasts," Staff Working Paper 2005-48, Federal Reserve Board

Kim, D., and Priebsch, M. (2013), "Estimation of Multi-Factor Shadow Rate Models," Working Paper in Progress, Federal Reserve Board, Washington D.C.

Kim, D., and Singleton, K. (2012), "Term Structure Models and the Zero Bound: An Empirical Investigation of Japanese Yields," *Journal of Econometrics*, 170(1):32–49

Krippner, L. (2012), "Modifying Gaussian Term Structure Models When Interest Rates are Near the Zero Lower Bound," Reserve Bank of New Zealand Discussion Paper 2012/02

Lund, J. (1997), "Non-Linear Kalman Filtering Techniques for Term Structure Models," Working Paper, Aarhus School of Business

Piazzesi, M. (2010), "Affine Term Structure Models," in *Handbook of Financial Econometrics*, ed. by Y. Aït-Sahalia, and L. P. Hansen. North-Holland, Amsterdam

Rosenbaum, S. (1961), "Moments of a Truncated Bivariate Normal Distribution," *Journal of the Royal Statistical Society*, 23(2):405–408

Severini, T. (2005), *Elements of Distribution Theory*, Cambridge Series in Statistical and Probabilistic Mathematics, Cambridge University Press

Wan, E., and van der Merwe, R. (2001), "The Unscented Kalman Filter," in *Kalman Filtering and Neural Networks*, ed. by S. Haykin, pp. 221–280

Wu, S. (2010), "Non-Linear Filtering in the Estimation of a Term Structure Model of Interest Rates," *WSEAS Transactions on Systems*, 9(7):724–733

www.ingramcontent.com/pod-product-compliance
Lightning Source LLC
Chambersburg PA
CBHW081808170526
45167CB00008B/3372